WALK
NEWHAVEN
CULTURAL HERITAGE TOURS

A PROJECT OF THE Ethnic Heritage Center

Use these QR code to access
this tour with a hand-held device

www.walknewhaven.org

The Ethnic Heritage Center
270 Fitch Street, New Haven, CT 06515
Phone: (203) 392-6126

http://ethnicheritagecenter.org/
E-mail: ethnicheritagecenter270@yahoo.com

ISBN: 978-0-9979091-1-1

To purchase copies of this and other Walk New Haven Guides,

visit www.walknewhaven.org/purchase.html.

COVER Pre-1945 Topo Map of New Haven 1890. Courtesy of the University of Texas Libraries, The University of Texas at Austin.

Contents

Downtown : Church & Chapel Streets

Downtown North : Orange Street & Hillhouse Avenue

SPONSORS

PLATINUM SPONSORS | $10,000 +
Jewish Foundation and Jewish Federation of Greater New Haven

GOLD SPONSORS | $2,000 – $9,999
Italian American Historical Society of Connecticut
Knights of Columbus
Jewish Historical Society of Greater New Haven
Irish History Round Table
Rosa DeLauro
Rita A. Landino

SILVER SPONSORS | $200 – $1,999
Carole Brown
Robert Larkin
Carol Burke
Rosemary Barrett
Patricia Heslin

FRIENDS | $20 – $199

John R. Amore
Patricia Lucan
Arnold Jewelers
Carol L. Cangiano
Lamberti Packing Company
Calabresi Foundation
Goodcopy Printing Center, Inc.
Greater New Haven African American Historical Society
Vincent & Mary McMahon
Richard & Margaret Hopkins
Maureen Condron Delahunt
Vito & Louise Cedro

Lee & Lillian Liberman
John & Kathleen O'Donovan
Sisk Brothers Funeral Home, Inc.
Celentano Funeral Home
Pietrina Sappern
Alfonsina Improta
Mike & Katie Regan
Joan Flood Ciaburri
Mary A. Wallace
Neil Hogan
Jean & Mary Anne Mauro
Anthony C. Passarello

Grace Brady
Gayle Logan
Richard & Neva Slattery
Nancy Coppola
Regina Barbaresi
Paul & Joan Weber
Patricia M. Wallace
Irving & Harriet Calechman
Joseph J. O'Brien
David M. Lynch
Daniel Kirby
Dominic Schioppo Jr.
Michael P. Sullivan

Introduction

This *Walk New Haven: Cultural Heritage Tours* guide is part of a series that has been created by the Ethnic Heritage Center (EHC). Although some of the buildings described are no longer standing, their stories remain. This self-guided walking/biking/driving tour tells the pre-1970 stories of the experiences, contributions and hardships faced in New Haven by five of the cultural and ethnic groups that have enriched our community. A major goal of the EHC is to stimulate an interest among the many additional cultural groups in New Haven to form historical societies to preserve and share their histories. This book is part of that process. We plan future volumes and a flexible project website (www.walknewhaven.org) prepared to include additional sites important to our cultural groups. The EHC was founded in 1988 and has five member historical societies:

- Jewish Historical Society of Greater New Haven, founded in 1976
- Italian-American Historical Society of Connecticut, founded in 1979
- Connecticut Ukrainian-American Historical Society, founded in 1983
- Connecticut Irish-American Historical Society, founded in 1988
- Greater New Haven African American Historical Society, founded in 2003

The EHC has been located on the campus of Southern Connecticut State University since 1992, where the archives of most of the societies are preserved. This project has been funded by a matching grant from the Jewish Foundation and Jewish Federation of Greater New Haven and by many local donors listed on the back of this book.

The sites on this tour are only a few of many such sites scattered throughout New Haven. The Ethnic Heritage Center encourages the public to share information and memories about our tour sites and additional sites, as well as to notify us of any inaccuracies, by contacting the EHC at 270 Fitch Street, New Haven CT 06515 or ethnicheritagecenter270@yahoo.com.

Cultural Heritage Overview of Downtown New Haven

Since 1640, the New Haven Green and its surrounding streets have been the center of New Haven's cultural, religious, and commercial life. This concentration of public functions and spaces in the city's downtown brought together citizens from diverse cultural backgrounds, despite the obstacles created by racial and religious discrimination. These two walking tours, Downtown (Church and Chapel Streets, see Tour Map, pp. 8–9) and Downtown North (Orange Street and Hillhouse Avenue, see Tour Map, pp. 32–33), will highlight examples of sites that reflect the pre-1970 experiences and contributions of the five cultural groups that are currently members of the Ethnic Heritage Center. Additional downtown tours are listed on the WALK NEW HAVEN website.

New Haven's first settlers were Puritans from England led by Theophilus Eaton and John Davenport. They established the original nine squares of their planned Christian utopia near settlements of the indigenous Quinnipiac people, who brought deer meat and wares to the New Haven Green to trade with the colonists. Even after a reservation for the natives was established on the eastern shore of the harbor, the Quinnipiacs and colonists continued meeting in the nine squares for commerce and political negotiation. These inter-ethnic encounters were complex and sometimes exploitative: some Quinnipiacs were converted to Christianity and worshiped in local churches, while others were subjected to punishment by local courts, or even enslavement.

City Hall and Church Street from the New Haven Green, c. 1913.

Ethnic Diversity from Early Days

From the early days of the New Haven Colony, Blacks were present in the downtown area. Some were free, while others were enslaved to the local white elite. The Wadsworth map of 1748 records the presence of a free African-American farmer named Jethro living in the northeast quadrant of the nine squares. The African Ecclesiastical Society, later to become the Dixwell Avenue Congregational Church, was organized in 1820 and purchased a church on Temple Street four years later (Downtown, #13). At the same time, a community of free Blacks established itself on the eastern edge of downtown. New Haven's William "King" Lanson, a successful builder/contractor, owned a boarding house that was frequented by White and African American clientele.

Many important episodes in the *Amistad* story took place in downtown's public buildings between 1839 and 1842, including the African captives' imprisonment in the City jail. A memorial commemorating the Africans' struggle for freedom was erected in front of City Hall in 1992 (Downtown, #2). Downtown New Haven contains more than half a dozen sites on the Connecticut Freedom Trail, established in 1996 to recognize places associated with the abolitionist movement, civil rights movement, and African-Americans' struggle for freedom and dignity in Connecticut. The Exchange Building (Downtown, #8) is also a site on the Connecticut Freedom Trail. It housed the law office of Roger Sherman Baldwin when he represented the *Amistad* Africans and worked with John Quincy Adams in preparing their case before the United States Supreme Court, which decided on March 9, 1841 that the African captives were free.

The first known Jews in New Haven were the Sephardic Pinto brothers, Jacob and Solomon. The two brothers were prosperous merchants who fought in the Patriot Army during the Revolutionary War. Jacob Pinto's impressive home, the first brick house in the city, was located near the intersection of State Street and Grand Avenue at the edge of the nine squares. The home owned by Solomon's son William still stands on Orange Street (Downtown North, #1). The Young Men's Hebrew Association, which would become the Jewish Community Center, was founded in an office building at 200 Orange Street in 1913 (Downtown, #4). After several downtown moves, the Jewish Community Center built a new facility at 1156 Chapel Street (Downtown, #18), an expansive modern facility. The present site of the Jewish Community Center is in Woodbridge. The oldest Jewish congregation in the state, Congregation Mishkan Israel (Downtown North, #4), was officially established in 1843 when Connecticut law permitted non-Christian societies to organize. Since 1840, the congregation had met in private homes in downtown. In 1856 the congregation purchased the Court Street Meeting House of the Third Congregational Church, and remained there until 1897 when their Orange Street Synagogue was built. This continued an established pattern of re-use of religious buildings that was repeated throughout the city's history as demographics and community needs shifted over time.

Irish immigrants initially arrived in New Haven as mariners and domestic servants, and by the 1820s significant numbers were drawn to the area as laborers for the Farmington Canal and the railroads. Initially settling in the "New Township" or Wooster Square neighborhood, many Irish came in the 1840s as a result of the potato famine. They settled in the Hill neighborhood, an area south of downtown known around 1800 as Sodom Hill and described as a place of poverty and crime, as well as in Fair Haven. The Irish established service businesses in the downtown as well as in the neighborhoods. They built the first Catholic Church in New Haven in 1834 and held New Haven's first St. Patrick's Day Parade in 1842 (Downtown, #5). About 90 members of the Hibernian Provident Society, a mutual aid organization, marched through the downtown streets behind a banner made especially for the occasion. The Knights of Columbus was founded in New Haven in 1882 to serve the city's Irish Catholic immigrant population. Its first offices were in Irish immigrant and Yale Law School graduate Cornelius Driscoll's law office at 157 Church Street (Downtown, #3).

Creating a Vibrant Community

New Haven's ethnic diversity was perhaps most clearly on display in downtown's many theaters and department stores. Many of these downtown establishments were owned by immigrant entrepreneurs. The Jewish-owned Shartenberg's department store (Downtown, #6), with its elegant Neoclassical six-storey building on Chapel Street, was one of the finest in New Haven. Irish immigrant Edward Malley founded a dry goods store in 1852 that became one of the city's premier retail outlets until closing in 1982 (Downtown, #12). Italian immigrant Sylvester Poli operated his theater empire, which extended across the entire northeastern United States, from his headquarters in New Haven. His Poli's Palace and Bijou Movie Theaters (Downtown, #10) on Church Street were among the largest and most beautiful movie theaters in the state. The Russian-Jewish Podoloff brothers completed construction of the New Haven Arena at Orange and Grove Streets in the 1920s (Downtown North, #2). For almost fifty years it hosted sporting events and musical concerts that drew New Haveners of all backgrounds. Other historic New Haven businesses launched by immigrant families included Kebabian's rug store, Del Monico's hat store, and Ferrucci Limited men's clothing on Elm Street. In the 19th century, there were several downtown German restaurants, and in the 20th and 21st centuries additional ethnic groups have brought their food to downtown

diners, including Chinese, Greek, Indian and Latino restaurants. A Puerto Rican Festival has become an annual August event on the Green, and there is currently an Ecuadorian Consulate on Church near George Street.

Originally a bastion of white Anglo-Saxon Protestant privilege, Yale University has become a place for high-achieving students of all ethnic and religious backgrounds. The world-renowned Ivy League university was founded in 1701 and moved to downtown New Haven from Saybrook, Connecticut in 1717. German-Jewish immigrant Sigmund Waterman graduated from Yale in the 1840s, the first Jew to do so (Downtown North, #7). Native New Havener Edward Bouchet was an early African American graduate of Yale and the first African American to earn a PhD in the United States. Unfortunately, discrimination against Jews, Blacks and other ethnic groups persisted well into the 20th century. In 2016 Yale named one of its new residential colleges after African-American civil rights activist Pauli Murray, making it the first Yale residential college to be named after a person of color.

Since its earliest days New Haven's downtown core has been the place where members of different religious and ethnic groups would come together in the practice of politics, commerce, recreation, and every other facet of life and death. People of varied backgrounds conducted business together in local markets and commercial establishments, engaged each other in political debate at City Hall, fought each other in legal disputes at the courthouse, encountered each other at public libraries and restaurants, and were even buried beneath the New Haven Green (New Haven's first and only cemetery until the Grove Street Cemetery was established in 1796). More than any other part of the city, downtown expresses the complex and multi-layered ethnic history of the city.

In addition to providing religious, social and cultural support programs for themselves, members of these ethnic groups have participated actively in the civic and political life of the community. They have served as elected officials to the Board of Education, Board of Aldermen, and even as mayor. They have supported community-wide educational, cultural, health care, and charitable institutions. As new cultural groups join our community, they continue this history of contributing to the enrichment of New Haven.

View west of Chapel Street from State Street, c. 1865.

Downtown Site Map : Church & Chapel Streets

This map shows two types of historic sites in Downtown: Standing buildings (blue circles) and demolished buildings (gray squares). Current and former sites for the historic use described are indicated as such. These and additional historic sites in the area may be found at walknewhaven.org/tours/sites/downtown.html.

1 New Haven Green

2 165 CHURCH | **Amistad Memorial**

3 157 CHURCH | **Knights of Columbus' First Office** *(demolished)*

4 200 ORANGE | **Young Men's Hebrew Association** *(demolished)*

5 746 CHAPEL/THE STREET BUILDING | **First St. Patrick's Day Parade 1842**

6 761 CHAPEL | **Shartenberg's Department Store** *(demolished)*

7 760 CHAPEL | **Horowitz Brothers** *(former)*

7 770–774 CHAPEL | **Mendel and Freedman** *(former)*

8 123 CHURCH/THE EXCHANGE BUILDING | **The Downes News Company** *(former)*

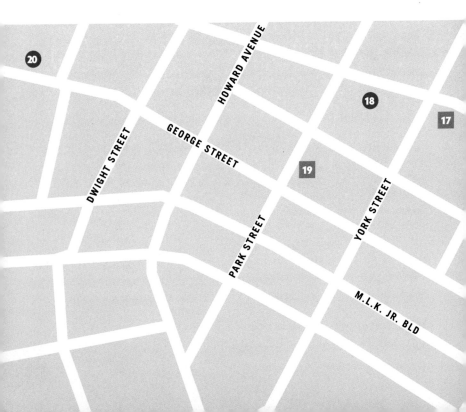

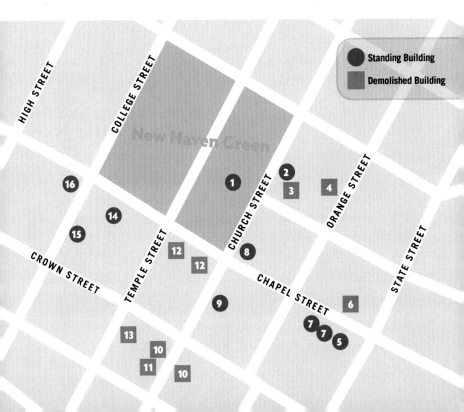

1

New Haven Green

The New Haven Green is a National Historic Landmark that has been at the center of life in New Haven since its boundaries were established in 1640. The Puritans founded New Haven Colony in 1638, and in 1640 surveyor John Brockett laid out a nine square city plan to the specifications of the founders. This central 16-acre public square was originally a communal marketplace and pasture and has been called the New Haven Green since 1779. In 1784, Temple Street was cut through the Green, creating two sections. The Garden Club of New Haven, in conjunction with the Proprietors of the Common and Undivided Lands in New Haven (who have legal responsibility for the Green), have created a free audio walking tour of the Green, available by dialing (203) 672-4384. They also published a brochure to accompany the audio tour, which is available online and at New Haven Visitor Centers (see #16 on this tour).

TOP *Postcard New Haven Green, c. 1920s.* BOTTOM *Current historic signage on the Green.*

2

165 CHURCH STREET

Amistad Memorial

The Amistad Memorial commemorates the history of the July 1, 1839 revolt led by Sengbe Pieh, known as Joseph Cinqué. Fifty-three kidnapped Mendeland West Africans, to be sold as slaves in Cuba, took over the vessel, La Amistad to return to Africa. When the ship dropped anchor off the coast of Long Island, the Africans were brought to the New Haven jail. They became the subject of landmark legal battles, eventually settled by the Supreme Court on March 9, 1841, which ruled that the Africans had been captured and transported illegally and were free. This stimulated the abolitionist movement in the United States.

The Amistad Memorial Foundation commissioned the Amistad Memorial for the City of New Haven, Connecticut in 1990. Sculpted by Edward Hamilton, this three-sided bronze monument stands on the former site of the New Haven Jail, where the kidnapped Africans were imprisoned in 1839 while awaiting trial. The three sides of the sculpture depict the capture, trial, and return to Mende of Joseph Cinqué and his thirty-four surviving compatriots. The Amistad Memorial was officially dedicated September 18, 1992.

The backdrop for this majestic 14-foot relief sculpture is New Haven's City Hall. The building façade is the only remaining portion of the Victorian Gothic-style City Hall building designed by Henry Austin and constructed c. 1861. The rear and north wings of the building were re-constructed in 1986.

LEFT Amistad Memorial. RIGHT *Painting of Sengbe Pieh, known as Joseph Cinqué displayed at the New Haven Museum.* BOTTOM *Keys to the New Haven Jail, c. 1839.*

157 CHURCH STREET

Knights of Columbus' First Office *(demolished)*
Cornelius Driscoll

Cornelius Driscoll was a lawyer, civic leader and New Haven's first immigrant Mayor. He was born in 1845 in County Cork, Ireland at the beginning of the devastating period in Irish history known as The Great Hunger (a.k.a. the Irish Famine 1845–1852). Driscoll and his family came to America c. 1850 and settled on a farm in Norwich Connecticut. Valedictorian of his class at Norwich Free Academy (Norwich, CT), Driscoll entered Yale in 1865, was admitted to practice law in Connecticut in 1870 and opened a law practice in New Haven. He was a founding member of the Knights of Columbus and the Order's first offices were housed in Driscoll's law office located directly to the right of City Hall at 157 Church Street. Driscoll served as a New Haven Alderman, Representative to the Connecticut General Assembly, New Haven Corporation Counsel and was New Haven's first immigrant Mayor (1899–1901). Driscoll's portrait is on display at New Haven City Hall.

LEFT *Official portrait of Mayor Driscoll, c. 1900.* RIGHT *157 Church Street, c. 1875.*

200 ORANGE STREET

Young Men's Hebrew Association *(demolished)*

The story of the Jewish Community Center of Greater New Haven (JCC) begins at this site with the founding of the Young Peoples' League in 1912. This organization, which changed its name to the Young Men's Hebrew Association, or YMHA, in 1913, held its meetings in a loft at 200 Orange Street. The Orange Street building also headquartered several of New Haven's charitable organizations, a fact which reflects the JCC's connection to charitable activities from early on.

In June 1915, the Young Women's Hebrew Association was formed. YWHA members organized activities including piano lessons, sewing and gymnastics. and often invited guest speakers from Yale University to their meetings at 301 George Street (home of Congregation Adas Israel, also known as "The Bolsheviki Shul"). The YMHA remained at Orange Street until 1918, when it purchased a one-family house at 304 Crown Street which would become its new headquarters. In 1921 the YWHA joined the YMHA on Crown Street, hired the first paid director to plan for the community, and finally had a building of its own. Space was limited and many felt it was time for a new modern building. The new era finally began in 1935, when the YMHA and YWHA merged to become the Jewish Community Center, headquartered at 7 Dwight Street, a building contributed by the Hebrew Institute. The JCC moved to Chapel Street in 1954 (Downtown, #18), then to Woodbridge in 1993.

YMHA occupied a loft in this United Workers and Organized Charities Building, c. 1914.

5

746 CHAPEL STREET/THE STREET BUILDING

First St. Patrick's Day Parade 1842

The first St. Patrick's Day Parade in New Haven was held March 17, 1842 when 90 members of the Hibernian Provident Society, a mutual aid organization formed the previous year, and one band marched through city streets behind a banner made especially for the occasion. The two mottos inscribed on the banner displayed the dual loyalties of the marchers: "E Pluribus Unum" and "Erin go Bragh" (Ireland forever). The event was at once a public affirmation of how much these immigrants cherished their traditions and the strength of their determination to become an accepted part of their new homeland. Today, New Haven's St. Patrick's Day parade is the sixth longest running parade in the U.S. and has grown into the largest single-day spectator event in Connecticut. In 1999, as part of the Library of Congress' 200th anniversary, the New Haven St. Patrick's Day Parade was selected as "A Local Legacies Project" and its history is preserved in the Library of Congress.

TOP *New Haven Parks Commission Float 1956 Parade.* BOTTOM *Historic St. Patrick's Day postcards.*

761 CHAPEL STREET

Shartenberg's Department Store *(demolished)*

Jacob S. Shartenberg, a Jewish immigrant from Germany in 1853, came to America at age sixteen and became an apprentice watchmaker. Later he was hired into the dry goods business and in 1881 started his own store in Pawtucket, Rhode Island, the New Idea Store.

In 1906 Shartenberg and his partner Henry Robinson bought Howe & Stetson Co. in New Haven. In 1913 Robinson left, and Shartenberg's sons Charles and Henry joined the business. Shartenberg opened a new building on Chapel Street in 1915. It had white pillars, six stories, and 150,000 square feet of floor space. Its doors opened onto Chapel, Orange and State Streets. It was the biggest department store in old downtown New Haven.

The department store came under new management in 1952, and business slowed in the recessions of 1958–59 and 1960. Shartenberg's finally closed in 1962, and was demolished in 1966 as part of Urban Renewal to make room for a then-planned parking facility. Today, 360 State Street Apartments, part of the current boom in downtown residential development, stands on the site.

TOP *Chapel Street, c. 1940s.* BOTTOM LEFT *Roadside billboard, c. 1926.*
BOTTOM RIGHT *Shartenberg's Department Store, c. 1915.*

7

760 CHAPEL STREET

Horowitz Brothers *(former)*

770-774 CHAPEL STREET

Mendel and Freedman *(former)*

The Chapel Street Horowitz Brothers building dates to the 1800s, and first housed dry goods retailer Charles Monson Co. William Horowitz, who was born in Russia in 1892, came to New Haven in 1910 and became a peddler. He was the founder and President of Horowitz Brothers, a dry goods store on Grand Avenue, which opened in 1913. His sons Phillip and Leonard and their cousin Arthur moved the store to Chapel Street in 1939. Phillip Horowitz and his employees were known for their friendliness. Phillip, Leonard and Arthur ran Horowitz Brothers for 66 years, until the store closed in early 2005 after Phillip's death. Monson Building LLC bought the building from the Horowitz family in January 2005. The southwest corner of Chapel and State Streets was renamed as the Horowitz Brothers Corner that April.

Adolph Mendel and Isidor Freedman, who was born in Bruckhausen, Germany in 1854, formed a business partnership, establishing what would become one of the biggest department stores in Connecticut. The number of employees grew from two clerks to 250 employees. The interior of the store was destroyed by a major fire and closed in 1921. Mr. Mendel formed a partnership with Mr. Harris and rebuilt the store as Mendel and Harris. When competition forced them to close, they were replaced by Stanley Dry Goods, which occupied the building for many years.

TOP LEFT *Horowitz Brothers, c. 1966.* TOP RIGHT *Trolley and Motorcars in front of Mendel and Freedman Department Store, c. 1918.* BOTTOM *Postcard of Mendel and Freedman, c. 1910.*

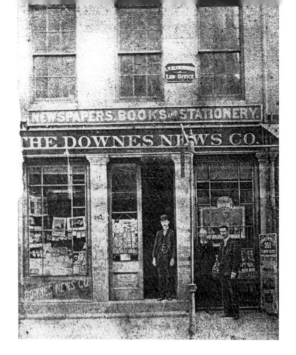

8

123 CHURCH STREET/THE EXCHANGE BUILDING

The Downes News Company *(former)*

Michael and Bridget Kenney Downes and their two-year-old son William emigrated to the U.S. from Ireland in 1827. They settled in New Haven in 1832. Michael Downes was New Haven's first news dealer, selling local and New York papers on the street and later from a shop on Church Street. For two cents patrons could sit in the shop's back room and read the New York papers. When Michael died in 1845 his two elder sons, eighteen-year-old William and sixteen-year-old Edward, took over the news shop, which was primarily operated by Edward. William soon took up the trade of bookbinding and with a partner opened a bookbinding business on Chapel Street near Orange Street. Edward Downes was the sole owner of the News Company from 1852 to 1873. In 1850 he moved the shop to the Exchange Building, a Greek-Revival building built in 1832. The firm experienced reorganizations and partnerships within the family before being dissolved in 1891. Edward's sons Alfred and Edward Jr. were graduates of Yale Law School and Edward Jr. served as New Haven's City Clerk and as the State Department's Consul General to Amsterdam before entering the priesthood, resuming a vocation he had abandoned to take care of his mother and siblings when his father died.

Storefront, c. 1870s.

9

81-85 CHURCH STREET

J. Johnson & Sons *(former)*

J. Johnson & Sons, Inc., founded in 1869, sold fine men's clothing. At one point it employed 65 people, and called itself The Live Store. Its founder Joseph Johnson was a noted community philanthropist who headed the fundraising committee to build a new Jewish Home for Children at 701 Sherman Avenue, to house and care for homeless Jewish children. He had studied violin with Harry Berman, who enlisted his support in 1930 to create the Johnson Junior Symphony, a children's orchestra. The Johnson Junior Symphony initially used space on the top floor of the store, sharing space with the tailors who altered the clothing. The youth orchestra was later taken over by his son, James S. Johnson, who kept it going for twenty-six years. The building was sold to Kennedy's, a subsidiary of the Phillips Van Heusen Co., in 1964, and the name changed to J. Johnson's–Kennedy's. In 1966 it moved its headquarters store to the Chapel Square Mall, where the name was shortened to Kennedy's. A decade later it was losing money, only employed 15 people, and eventually closed. Near the top of the original building on Church Street, the engraving J. Johnson and Sons remains today.

J. Johnson & Sons, c. 1950s.

S. Z. Poli, Prop.

26 CHURCH STREET

Poli's Bijou Theater *(demolished)*

Sylvester Zefferino (S. Z.) Poli was born in Bolognana, Gallicano, Lucca, Tuscany, Italy in 1858. Soon after, his family moved to neighboring Piano di Coreglia. He came to America in 1881 with little more than the ability to carve lifelike figures from wax, a skill gained through apprenticeship under French sculptor M. Dublex, and parlayed his talents into a grand theatrical empire in his adopted home of New Haven. In 1885 while working in New York, S. Z. met and married Rosa Leverone of Genoa, Italy, and together they had five children.

The Polis settled in New Haven in 1892 and S. Z. opened Poli's Eden Musée which featured wax figures he had created in Italy. In 1893, Poli's Wonderland Theater was opened in a building originally used as a church and until 1874, was the location of St. Mary's Church (#11 on this tour). This proved to be the start of one of the largest and most lucrative chains of East Coast vaudeville and movie theaters. It was at the Wonderland that Poli showed the first motion pictures in New Haven using the French cinemagraph. In 1907, the 1,430 seat Bijou Theater, considered to be an outstanding example of theater architecture in its day, opened. Players like Houdini, Sophie Tucker and George M. Cohan performed for large audiences in Poli's magnificent theaters throughout the Northeast.

Postcard of Bijou Theater, c. 1910.

23 CHURCH STREET

Poli's Palace Theater *(demolished)*

By 1905 Poli built the new Palace Theater across Church Street from the Wonderland. In order to stay competitive, the Poli Palace was gutted and re-opened in 1917 with seating for 3,005 and featured Mickey Rooney and Judy Garland live in August, 1939. It had a Moller organ and a marble staircase leading to business offices above the theater, including Poli's Theatrical Enterprises and other professional offices pertaining to arts and culture. One such office was occupied by piano teacher and voice coach, Marie Gagliardi Fiengo, who attended the Julliard School of Music and was well known in the New Haven area.

By 1916 S. Z. Poli was the world's largest individual theater owner. Movie theaters flourished during Hollywood's golden age and the Poli Palace and Bijou were no exceptions. The Italian immigrant population of New Haven, along with residents throughout the area, frequented both movie theaters which offered them a respite from their long work hours, at a reasonable cost of approximately 25 cents per movie as late as the 1930s. In 1928, Poli sold his theaters to Fox New England Theatres, retaining 3/4 interest and creating Fox-Poli's. With the stock market crash of 1929, Fox lost the theaters which reverted back to Poli. Poli retired in 1934 and sold his theaters to the Loew's Theatre chain (founded in 1904 by Marcus Loew). The theaters became known as the Loew's Poli Theaters.

Sylvester and Rosa were popular community leaders who supported local and international charities, raising money for the war effort and the Red Cross. Sylvester Poli spent his final years at his summer home, the Villa Rosa (named after his wife) in Woodmont, Connecticut. The family's former home, a sumptuous mansion, still exists on the corner of Forest Road and upper Chapel.

LEFT *Military parade marching past Poli's Vaudeville Theater, 1908.* RIGHT *Sylvester Poli, 1920.*

22 CHURCH STREET

First St. Mary's R.C. Church *(demolished)*

From 1848 to 1874 this location was home to New Haven's first (and Connecticut's second) Catholic parish. Prior to 1829 when the Rev. Bernard O'Cavanagh took up residence in Hartford, Connecticut's Catholics were ministered to by itinerant priests from Boston and Providence. Services were held in private homes, barns and occasionally in a church of another denomination. In 1832 the Rev. James McDermot was assigned to New Haven as its first resident priest. In 1834 Fr. McDermot and his approximately 200 mainly Irish congregants established the state's second Catholic parish—Christ's Church, located at the corner of York St. and Davenport Ave. This official arrival of "Popery" was greeted with fear and suspicion, and less than six months after its dedication Christ's Church was broken into, the altar stripped of its ornaments, and the crucifix and silver chalice stolen. In an encouraging and welcoming gesture, non-Catholics joined together to replace the chalice. The story of Christ's Church as such came to a devastating end in June 1848 when the church was totally destroyed by what was believed to be a deliberately set fire. Services were held in a tent until December when a Congregational Meeting House on Church St. was purchased and refitted for Catholic worship. Renamed St. Mary's, it was dedicated in December 1848. St. Mary's remained on Church St. until moving to Hillhouse Avenue in 1874 when the current church was completed (see Downtown North tour, #8). As the successor to Christ's Church, St. Mary's is still considered to be the second oldest Catholic parish in Connecticut. In 1858, a new church was built at the former Christ's Church location on Davenport Avenue. Named St. John the Evangelist, it was the first church in the United States to be built in the Celtic style of architecture, which had prevailed throughout Ireland during the 11th and 12th centuries.

LEFT *Chalice donated by non-Catholics in 1835 as replacement for one stolen from Christ's Church.*
RIGHT *St. Mary's Church, center, Bailey and Hazen Aerial Map, 1878.*

902 CHAPEL STREET

Edw. Malley Co. *(demolished)*

890 CHAPEL STREET

Gamble-Desmond's *(demolished)*

One of downtown New Haven's landmark buildings and prestigious department stores, Malley's was founded by Irish immigrant Edward Malley in 1852. The store's roots were in Malley's aunt's front room in Fair Haven where Malley first displayed his merchandise. His first store was a 300-sq. ft. dry goods store located across from the New Haven Green, with deliveries made from a cart pulled by a mule named Maude. By 1856 the store had expanded to 9,000 sq. ft. and employed 100 people. For nearly 70 years The Edw. Malley Co. was located in a nine-storey Beaux-Arts style building at the corner of Chapel and Temple Streets. The store was relocated to 2 Church Street (now the site of Gateway Community College) in the 1960s to allow construction of the Chapel Square Mall. A family business until 1971, Malley's survived ownership by several different retailers until 1982.

Edw. Malley Co., c. 1871.

One of Malley's early employees was another Irish immigrant, David S. Gamble. Gamble worked at Malley's for 21 years as a salesman and superintendent. In 1883 Gamble left Malley's to become superintendent at F.M. Brown & Co., a dry goods house right next door to Malley's on Chapel Street. In 1898 Gamble joined with Irish immigrant John D. Desmond to form a new company which purchased F.M. Brown. The Gamble-Desmond Company joined the Edw. Malley Company as one of New Haven's prestigious department stores, also replaced by the Chapel Square Mall.

TOP *Edw. Malley Co., c. 1890.* BOTTOM LEFT *Gamble-Desmond's, c. 1915.* BOTTOM RIGHT *Both stores, c. 1882.*

105 TEMPLE STREET

Temple Street Congregational Church and B'nai Jacob Synagogue (demolished)

In 1820, Blacks in New Haven were relegated at worship to the balcony of the First Congregational Church, located on the New Haven Green. A group of Black worshippers persuaded Simeon Smith Jocelyn (1799–1879) a white abolitionist and Yale student, to conduct religious services with them at his home. Four men and eighteen women, including Bias Stanley, Dorcas Lanson, Nicholas Cisco, and Adeline Cooper, came together as the first Black congregation in New Haven.

In 1824, the congregation organized as the African Ecclesiastical Society and purchased a building at 105 Temple Street. On August 25, 1829, the Western Association of New Haven County formally recognized the Temple Street Congregational Church and ordained Simeon Jocelyn as its minister. He served in that position until 1834.

Other noted pastors of the Temple Street Church included James W. C. Pennington, a former slave, noted orator, writer and abolitionist who wrote what is considered the first history of Blacks in the United States, "The Origin and History of the Colored People" (1841). The Rev. Amos G. Beman, pastor of the Temple Street Church from 1838 to 1857, was a noted temperance lecturer, anti-slavery agitator, agent and station master of the Underground Railway, and tireless worker for Negro Suffrage in Connecticut. His papers and scrapbooks are archived in the Beinecke Rare Book and Manuscript Library at Yale University.

The Rev. Albert President Miller was pastor of the Temple Street Congregational Church when the congregation purchased the old North Church Mission Chapel at 100 Dixwell Avenue and moved there in 1886. The Temple Street building was sold in 1885 to Congregation B'nai Jacob, founded in 1882 by Jewish immigrants from Russia. It continued in use until 1912, when the congregation moved to a new synagogue erected at 347 George Street.

Temple Street Congregational Church and B'nai Jacob Synagogue, c. 1910.

14

962-964 CHAPEL STREET

First Knights of Columbus Headquarters *(former)*

In 1904, Chapel Street between Temple and College was transitioning to retail and office uses. A lot at 956 Chapel Street was where the Knights of Columbus chose to build its "first real home." The Orders' Supreme Office or headquarters had been in New Haven since its founding by Fr. Michael McGivney in 1882, but had previously occupied leased space at 157 Church Street (the offices of incorporators Daniel Colwell and Cornelius T. Driscoll), the Hoadley Building (corner of Church and Crown Streets) and the Poli Building (21–23 Church Street). Architect Lyman Faxon was selected to design a four storey modern French Renaissance-style building containing retail space on the first floor, office space for lease by professionals on the second and third floors, and club rooms and general offices for the Order on the third and fourth floors. The building was dedicated on June 6, 1906; the invocation was given by Rev. P.J. McGivney, K of C National Chaplain and Fr. Michael McGivney's brother. It served as the Order's Headquarters until 1922. The lot to the west became the Bohan-Landorf Co. building, a retail establishment owned in part by first generation Irish-American Michael Bohan.

Building decorated for Dedication and K of C National Convention June 6, 1906.

15

247 COLLEGE STREET

Shubert Theater

Maurice Bailey

The Shubert Theater was opened in 1914 by the Shubert Brothers and named in memory of their deceased brother, Sam S. Shubert. It was designed by architect Albert Swazey of New York and seated 1500 people. The first show was "The Belle of Bond Street" starring Broadway comedian Sam Bernard. Seats for the opening engagement were priced from 25 cents to $1.50. From its very first season, the Shubert Theatre has been a performing arts center presenting plays, musicals, opera, dance, classical music recitals and concerts, vaudeville, jazz artists, big bands, burlesque, and a variety of solo performances. The Shubert brothers ran the theater from 1914 through the 1940-41 season, establishing the pattern of try-outs. Of the fourteen musicals in the first season, four were new shows that played the Shubert before opening in New York. The theater was re-opened in 1941 by a New Haven corporation headed by Maurice H. Bailey who owned several motion pictures theaters, including the Whalley Theater, which he had opened in the 1920s. His parents had been Russian Jewish immigrants, and his father died when Maurice was twelve years old. The Shubert quickly became the theater of choice to try out new productions drawing many famous performers, writers, directors and producers, including almost all of the Rodgers & Hammerstein musicals, and became known as "The Birthplace of the Nation's Greatest Hits." From its original mission as a Broadway tryout house, the theater has evolved into the Shubert Performing Arts Center, a not-for-profit community resource that serves as the heartbeat of the region's cultural life.

Maurice Bailey also contributed to the community as a leader on the New Haven Board of Finance, as Chairman of the Board of the Jewish Home for the Aged and as Building Chair for Congregation B'nai Jacob when their new Woodbridge synagogue was built, opening in 1961.

LEFT *Maurice Bailey, c. 1947.* RIGHT *Shubert Theater, c. 1930s.*

16

1000 CHAPEL STREET

Townsend Block *(New Haven Visitor Information)*

This is one of three commercial Greek Revival style buildings built in the 1830s which remain on Chapel Street. The other two are the Exchange Building (#8 on this tour, corner of Church Street) and the Street Building (#5 on this tour, corner of State Street). Before these were built, the shops along Chapel Street had looked like houses with storefronts. The Townsend Building now houses the New Haven Visitor Information Center, which has brochures and flyers about additional cultural sites, stores, tours and special events in the City. The building is also the home of Claire's Corner Copia, a popular vegetarian restaurant founded by Claire LaPia Criscuolo and her late husband Frank Criscuolo on September 17, 1975.

Townsend Block, c. 1892.

1110 CHAPEL STREET

WNHC TV *(demolished)*
Patrick J. Goode and Aldo DeDominicis

When young Patrick Goode arrived from Galway, Ireland, with his parents, sister and 3 brothers, neither he nor his parents could have envisioned his future in New Haven. In a career spanning 60 years, Patrick worked as a mail carrier, and as private secretary to Connecticut Congressman Thomas Reilly, New Haven Postmaster Philip Troup and S. Z. Poli in his theatrical business. While Patrick was in charge of the Poli Theater real estate department from 1920 to 1934, he organized WELI, the first of his two local radio stations. Patrick Goode served as New Haven Postmaster from 1936 to 1950. In 1934, Patrick and Italian immigrant Aldo DeDominicis, of Abruzzi, Italy, established WNHC radio, and in 1948 WNHC TV (Channel 6). This was the first television station in Connecticut and Southern New England. Aldo DeDominicis had been a successful pasta salesman and had also sold air time on WELI radio for Italian programs. He believed in TV and convinced the DuMont television network to give him equipment to start a station. The WNHC television station broadcast from the radio station's building at 1110 Chapel Street. The station was the first in the country to use videotape for local programming and one of the first to broadcast in color and create local TV shows such as Connecticut Bandstand. In 1971 the station's call letters were changed to WTNH-TV and it now broadcasts on Channel 8. The station moved to its present location at State and Elm Streets, c. 1984.

TOP *WNHC-TV Studio, 1952*. BOTTOM LEFT *Patrick J. Goode, c. 1950*. BOTTOM RIGHT *Aldo DeDominicis, c. 1931*.

18

1156 CHAPEL STREET

Jewish Community Center *(former)*

The Jewish Community Center (JCC) held a ground-breaking ceremony on June 1, 1952 on this site. The new Center, an early work of famed architect Louis Kahn, was completed in 1954. The JCC flourished on Chapel Street and became the cornerstone of an upper Chapel Street revitalization. Then, as now, a strong membership was key to its success. Thousands of people's lives were touched by hours spent at the Chapel Street JCC. Its many features included a teen lounge, a basement woodworking shop, summer day camp on the roof, a swimming pool, a health club, and bowling lanes.

By 1976, however, use of the downtown facility was in decline. At that time much of its membership had already moved north and west to the suburbs, and earlier the adjacent Legion Avenue neighborhood, previously home to much of New Haven's Jewish community, had been razed. In 1982, the Chapel Street facility was placed on the market and the JCC began making plans for a move. The building was sold in 1985 and programs were housed in leased facilities until the new JCC in Woodbridge opened in November, 1993. The building now houses the Yale University School of Art.

Jewish Community Center at 1156 Chapel Street, c. 1960s.

125 PARK STREET

St. Michael the Archangel Ukrainian Catholic Church
(demolished)

20

563 GEORGE STREET

St. Michael the Archangel Ukrainian Catholic Church and Ukrainian National Home

St. Michael the Archangel Ukrainian Catholic Church began in 1909 in a house in Fair Haven. There had been a Ukrainian community in New Haven for approximately twenty years when the property at 125 Park Street was purchased in 1911 as the site for its first church. The church building had been home to St. Luke's Episcopal Church, a congregation of predominantly African-Americans, from 1852 to 1905, and then to a Swedish Methodist Church. Named for St. Michael the Archangel, the "Little Grey Church on Park Street" was home to the congregation and the hub of the Ukrainian community until 1958.

On September 16, 1947, a large stone house and adjacent brick house at 555–563 George Street were purchased by the parish. They were used as a Ukrainian National Home, Ukrainian language school ("Ridna Shkola"), a meeting place

for the Ukrainian community's many organizations and residence for new immigrants. The Ukrainian National Home was organized in 1950 and initially leased space from St. Michael's Ukrainian Catholic Church at 563 George Street. In 1956 the Ukrainian National Home purchased a building at 162 Day Street which served as a meeting place and permanent home for many Ukrainian organizations.

In March 1957, the building at 569 George Street was razed and construction began for a new church, auditorium and classrooms. The facility was designed by Yastremski Architects and built by Joseph F. Kelly Company. In November 1958, the cornerstone was placed. By November 14, 1964, the mortgage was paid. In 1964, the house at 573 George Street next to the rectory was purchased for $40,000. The Heritage Center was opened in 1984. Its collections include artistic artifacts, historical documents and literary resources that serve not only to preserve a culture, but also to enable it to flourish. In 2009, the parish celebrated its 100th anniversary.

UPPER LEFT 125 Park Street, St. Michael the Archangel Ukrainian Catholic Church. LOWER LEFT *Immaculate Conception Society outside Park St. Church with Father Borsa, 1946.* RIGHT *Current Church on George Street.* TOP *Interior of George Street Church.* LOWER *Children from the Ridna Shkola at the former Ukrainian National Home at 162 Day Street, c. 1956.*

Downtown North Site Map : Orange Street & Hillhouse Avenue

This map shows two types of historic sites in Downtown North: Standing buildings (blue circles) and demolished buildings (gray squares). Current and former sites for the historic use described are indicated as such. These and additional historic sites in the area may be found at walknewhaven.org/tours/sites/downtownnorth.html.

1   275 ORANGE | **William Pinto House** *(former)*

2   10 – 40 GROVE | **New Haven Arena** *(demolished)*

3   352 ORANGE | **Maier Zunder House** *(former)*

4   380 ORANGE | **Mishkan Israel Synagogue** *(former)*

5   405 ORANGE | **Stephen J. Maher Residence** *(former)*

6   18 TRUMBULL | **Lafayette Mendel House** *(former)*

7   441 ORANGE | **Leopold Waterman House/Jewish Home for Children** *(former)*

8   5 HILLHOUSE | **St. Mary's Church**

9   15 HILLHOUSE | **Yale Collection of Musical Instruments**

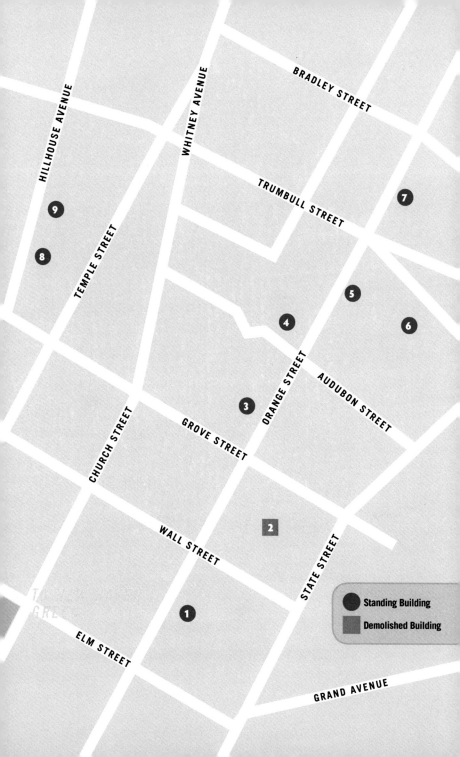

BRADLEY STREET

WHITNEY AVENUE

HILLHOUSE AVENUE

TRUMBULL STREET

TEMPLE STREET

9

8

7

5

4

6

ORANGE STREET

AUDUBON STREET

3

CHURCH STREET

GROVE STREET

WALL STREET

2

STATE STREET

● Standing Building

■ Demolished Building

1

ELM STREET

GRAND AVENUE

1

275 ORANGE STREET

William Pinto House *(former)*

This Federal-style house, built in 1810, is a link to some of the earliest Jews in New Haven. The brothers Jacob and Solomon Pinto, of Sephardic descent, arrived in New Haven around 1758. As prominent citizens they were acquainted with leading New Haveners of the day such as Roger Sherman, Noah Webster, Benedict Arnold, Eli Whitney, and Yale President Ezra Stiles. According to Stiles, the Pinto brothers did not practice Judaism and had "renounced all religion."

Jacob's son William graduated from Yale and immediately joined the Patriot Army in the Revolutionary War. As an officers' secretary, he became known for his penmanship and made copies of the Declaration of Independence for Connecticut Governor Jonathan Trumbull. Later, William was stationed in New London. When the British landed there in 1781 to burn the city, William was sent to deliver the news to Governor Trumbull at his war office in Lebanon. William's brothers Solomon and Abraham also fought for American independence. After the war, William became a merchant in the West Indies shipping trade and died in New Orleans in 1847. William Pinto acquired the house at 275 Orange Street from the original owner John Cook around 1815. Inventor Eli Whitney is believed to have died here in 1825 while staying with Pinto, as Whitney waited for construction to be completed on his own house across the street.

William Pinto House, c. 1930.

10 – 40 GROVE STREET

New Haven Arena *(demolished)*

One of the most important figures in the history of American sports got his start at this spot, on the southeastern corner of Orange and Grove Streets. Maurice Podoloff arrived from Elizabethgrad, Russia in 1890 when he was three months old. He and his brothers Nathan, Jacob and David all went to Yale. Maurice graduated from Yale in 1913, and in 1915 received a law degree. With his brother Nathan and father Abraham, Maurice took over the bankrupt, partially built New Haven Arena. He completed the construction with Nathan in 1927. Soon it became the leading venue in New Haven for hockey, basketball, boxing, wrestling and other sporting events. A local favorite was the annual arrival of the circus train, with the elephant parade up State Street from Union Station to the Arena. The Arena held over 4,000 people. The Arena hosted the American Hockey League's New Haven Eagles from 1936 to 1951, the New Haven Blades of the Eastern Hockey League from 1954 to 1972 and Yale Hockey from 1927 to 1959. They also featured orchestras from the Big Band era, such as Tommy and Jimmy Dorsey and Benny Goodman. Later, The Rolling Stones, the Kinks, Bob Dylan, The Doors, Joan Baez, the Supremes, the Temptations and many music icons held concerts at the Arena as well. Jacob Podoloff ran the Arena until 1972 when it was purchased by the City. It was replaced as a venue in 1973 by the New Haven Coliseum and the Arena was demolished in 1974.

Maurice brought professional hockey to New Haven. He was the head of the American Hockey League from the 1930s to 1952. He was also the president of the Basketball Association of America, and became the first president of the NBA when the BAA merged with the National Basketball League. He was later inducted into the National Basketball Hall of Fame. The NBA's Most Valuable Player award trophy is named in honor of Podoloff, who died in 1985 at the age of 95.

LEFT *Inaugural booklet from Grand Opening of the Arena.* RIGHT *New Haven Arena, c. 1951.*

3

352 ORANGE STREET

Maier Zunder House *(former)*

Maier Zunder (1829–1901) emigrated from Bavaria as a young man in 1848, fleeing from the German revolution and revolts of that year. He came to New Haven in 1852, following the death of his brother Samuel who had owned a grocery store at 54 Church Street. He turned the store into a large wholesale house, M. Zunder & Sons, which included groceries, especially imported foods from France and Germany, wines and brandies (until Prohibition in 1919), and tobacco. He soon became one of the leading entrepreneurs in the community. In 1866, he became one of the incorporators of the former Mechanics Bank, and was elected its President in 1872. He is credited with helping to establish two Jewish lodges in New Haven, the Horeb Lodge of B'nai B'rith for men and the Jochebed Lodge of the United Order of True Sisters for women. He was elected in 1868 to the New Haven Board of Education, where he served for twenty-four years, promoting bilingual education for immigrants, free school books, integrated schools and a curriculum that included the arts and physical education. He was honored by having a school named for him, the Zunder School (formerly located on George Street near College Street.) He also served as Treasurer for Congregation Mishkan Israel for twenty-five years and was active in numerous other community societies and organizations.

He owned two townhouses on Orange Street, numbers 348 and 352, and lived in one of them from 1860 to 1901. They are now combined and serve as a law office.

Maier Zunder House, 2016.

4

380 ORANGE STREET

Mishkan Israel Synagogue *(former)*

Mishkan Israel Synagogue, established in 1840, is the oldest synagogue in Connecticut. From 1840–1843 worship took place in a congregant's home. In 1843 the congregation's first official synagogue was dedicated on Grand Avenue. In 1856 the congregation purchased the Court Street Meeting House of the Third Congregational Church. Orthodox Congregants left to form B'nai Scholom Synagogue (see #22 in the Wooster Square Tour Book), while Mishkan Israel continued to follow Reform ritual. By 1894 Mishkan Israel's congregation was growing, and in 1897 an impressive new Temple with Spanish Renaissance-style architecture was dedicated on Orange Street. The synagogue moved to Ridge Road in 1960. In the 1960s Mishkan Israel's Rabbi Robert Goldberg was involved in liberal causes, including challenging McCarthyism, supporting the Civil Rights and Antiwar movements, and inviting Martin Luther King Jr. to speak at the Temple. He was even arrested in a civil rights gathering in Georgia. The ACES Educational Center for the Arts, a regional public after school program that provides high school students with the experience of studying the fine arts with practicing professional artists, now occupies the site, with the façade of the former Congregation Mishkan Israel preserved.

Mishkan Israel Synagogue, c. 1910.

5

Stephen J. Maher Residence *(former)*

The handsome row houses at 405–415 Orange Street were built c. 1864. The unit at number 405 (unit on extreme right) was the home for many years of Dr. Stephen J. Maher, a leading expert on tuberculosis. Dr. Maher's paternal grandparents immigrated to America in 1825 and his mother and her family came to this country in 1844. Dr. Maher was born in New Haven in 1860. The oldest of 8 sons, Dr. Maher was an 1887 honors graduate of Yale Medical School and did post-graduate work in hospitals in Ireland and England. Much of his career was devoted to the treatment of tuberculosis, particularly to isolating drugs effective in arresting complications of the disease. Dr. Maher oversaw construction of five state sanatoriums. Appointed to the state's Tuberculosis Commission in 1911, he was the only American physician to attend an international congress on TB, held in Germany in 1913. In 1906 Dr. Maher was one of the organizers of New Haven's Catholic Hospital Association (though not all members were Catholic) for the purpose of establishing the Hospital of St. Raphael (1908), a faith-based hospital where any doctor could offer care–and any person could be cared for–regardless of race, religion, culture or financial status.

LEFT *Dr. Maher, c. 1890.* RIGHT *Dr. Maher, c. 1933.*

6

18 TRUMBULL STREET

Lafayette Mendel House *(former)*

This Italianate house, designed by New Haven's greatest nineteenth century architect Henry Austin, was the home of scientist and Yale professor Lafayette Benedict Mendel from 1900 to 1924. Beginning in 1909, he conducted joint research with Thomas B. Osborne of the Connecticut Agricultural Experiment Station, discovering the nutritive value of proteins and vitamins, including the study of Vitamin A, Vitamin B, lysine and tryptophan.

He was one of the first tenured Jewish professors at Yale University and the first Jew to be named a Sterling Professor, Yale's most prestigious faculty appointment. He was the first president of the American Institute of Nutrition and was inducted into the National Academy of Sciences in 1913. The house was declared a National Historic Landmark in 1976.

Lafayette Mendel House, 2016.

7

Leopold Waterman House and Jewish Home for Children *(former)*

A Jewish immigrant from Bavaria in southern Germany, Leopold Waterman was the first president of Congregation Mishkan Israel. He was active in many local and national Jewish organizations, a founding member of B'nai B'rith, and corresponded with many of the leading Jewish and non-Jewish figures of his day, from Rabbi Isaac Mayer Wise to philosopher Ralph Waldo Emerson to Louis Kossuth, the Hungarian statesman and freedom fighter. Leopold served as Kossuth's translator when Kossuth came to Connecticut on a fundraising tour in 1851. Leopold's brother Sigmund was an instructor of German (his native language) and was probably the first Jew to teach at Yale. In 1848 Sigmund graduated from medical school at Yale and went on to a distinguished career in medicine. Leopold built this Greek Revival-style house in the 1840s. In 1905 the house became an orphanage for Jewish children. The Jewish Home for Children relocated to Sherman Avenue in 1924.

Leopold Waterman House, 2016.

8

5 HILLHOUSE AVENUE

St. Mary's Church

St. Mary's Church, successor to Christ's Church (1834) which was New Haven's first Catholic Church (Downtown, #11), was designed by James Murphy, an Irish immigrant from County Tipperary, and dedicated in 1874. The grave of Rev. Patrick Murphy, who finished the building of the church, is located at the front of the church, guarded by an iron gate; a memorial stone to Fr. Murphy is also imbedded in the outer wall of the church to the upper right of the grave. In 1878 Fr. Michael McGivney, the son of Irish immigrant parents, was assigned to St. Mary's as a curate. In 1882, in the basement of St. Mary's, Fr. McGivney and his mostly working-class Irish parishioners founded the Knights of Columbus, a fraternal benefit society formed to protect the widows and children of working men and to foster faith and social progress. In 1982, on the 100th anniversary of the founding of the K of C, Fr. McGivney's remains were re-interred from his native Waterbury to a sarcophagus at the rear nave of St. Mary's. The church's spire, part of the original design but not constructed due to financial constraints, was donated by the Knights of Columbus in 1986. New Haven continues to be the home of the K of C, whose International Headquarters are at 1 Columbus Plaza, Church Street.

TOP *St. Mary Church, c. 1875.* BOTTOM *Fr. McGivney and the founders of the Knights of Columbus, c. 1880s.*

9

15 HILLHOUSE AVENUE

Yale Collection of Musical Instruments

Morris Steinert

Born in 1831, Moritz (later Morris) Steinert was a Bavarian Jew who immigrated to the United States in 1850. He was living in Georgia in 1861 when the start of the American Civil War led to his relocation to New Haven. Through his acquaintance with piano manufacturer and fellow German immigrant William Steinway, Steinert became a distributor of Steinway Pianos. By the 1880s M. Steinert & Sons was one of the most successful piano dealerships in New England. The company still exists today, based in Boston. Combining his musical and philanthropic interests, Steinert founded the New Haven Symphony in 1894. A talented multi-instrument musician himself (he played piano, organ, flute, cello, and violin), Steinert was one of the original members of the orchestra. Steinert was also an avid collector of rare and antique instruments. His collection was donated to Yale in 1900, and became the early core of the Yale Collection of Musical Instruments.

TOP *Building housing the Yale Collection of Musical Instruments, 2016.* BOTTOM *Morris Steinert, c. 1890s.*

Acknowledgments

This project was initially made possible through the enthusiastic support of New Haven Mayor Toni Harp and a generous matching grant from the Jewish Foundation and Jewish Federation, with special thanks to Sydney Perry and Lisa Stanger. We appreciate the support of Dr. Mary A. Papazian, former President of Southern Connecticut State University which has provided a home to the Ethnic Heritage Center since 1992. Patrick Cardon of *The Museum in the Streets* was very encouraging and generous with his time in our initial planning. We thank Jason Bischoff-Wurstle (Photo Archivist) and Margaret Ann Tockarshewsky (Director) of the *New Haven Museum,* Anne Ostendarp of the *Knights of Columbus Multimedia Archive* and local historians Joe Taylor and Colin Caplan for sharing their historic pictures and insights. We also thank Martha Sullivan for help with proofreading, and Angel Diggs from the *New Haven Register* and Seth Godfrey and Allison Botelho from the *New Haven Free Public Library* for research assistance. Special thanks to Allen Samuel for his ongoing technical and moral support.

Jewish Historical Society of Greater New Haven: Rhoda Sachs Zahler Samuel (Project Coordinator), Robert Pierce Forbes, Ph.D. (Historian and Copy Editor), Marvin Bargar (JHS Archivist), Michael Berson (Student Intern), Albert Harary (President), Aaron Goode, Judith Schiff (City of New Haven Historian and Chief Research Archivist at Yale's Sterling Library), Patricia B. Illingworth (Office Administrator), Judith Janette, Edith Goodmaster

Greater New Haven African American Historical Society: Margery Mills, Valerie Bertrand (President), Diane Petaway, Edward Cherry, FAIA, Tarah Cherry, Sheila Jewell

Italian-American Historical Society of Connecticut: Joanne Iuteri Ludwig (Vice President), Jane Scarpellino, Jo-Anne Giammattei, Maria Villecco, Patricia Esposito, Frances Calzetta

Connecticut Irish-American Historical Society: Patricia Heslin, Tom Geirin, Paul Keroack, Susan Brosnan, George Waldron (President), Maureen Delahunt

Connecticut Ukrainian-American Historical Society: Gloria Horbaty, Donald Horbaty

Ethnic Heritage Center: Frank James Andriulli III (SCSU Student Intern)

Design and Project Consultant: Jeanne Criscola, *Criscola Design*

Credits

PAGE 6-9 Photos courtesy of Joe Taylor and New Haven Museum. Text source: Ethnic Heritage Center, Aaron Goode.

PAGE 12 Postcard courtesy of Joe Taylor. Text source: Garden Club of New Haven, *Walking Tour of the Historic New Haven Green*.

PAGE 13 Photos courtesy of New Haven Museum and Allen Samuel. Text source: Amistad Memorial Foundation.

PAGE 14 Photograph by Joseph K. Bundy courtesy of Colin M. Caplan. Portrait source: www. publicartarchive.org. Text source: *The Shanachie* Vol. XXV No. 1, 2013, CT Irish American Historical Society Newsletter.

PAGE 15 Photo courtesy of New Haven Museum. Text source: Jewish Historical Society of Greater New Haven Archives.

PAGE 16 Photos courtesy of CT Irish American Historical Society Archives: Collection of Richard Clark and *St. Patrick's Day Parade A Local Legacies Project*. Text source: *The Wearin' o' the Green St. Patrick's Day in New Haven CT 1842-1992* by Neil Hogan.

PAGE 17 Photos courtesy of New Haven Museum, Jewish Historical Society of Greater New Haven Archives and Joe Taylor. Text source: Jewish Historical Society of Greater New Haven Archives.

PAGE 18 Photos courtesy of Jewish Historical Society of Greater New Haven and New Haven Museum; postcard courtesy of Joe Taylor. Text source: Jewish Historical Society of Greater New Haven Archives.

PAGE 19 Photo and text source: Paul Keroack.

PAGE 20 Postcard courtesy of Joe Taylor. Text source: Jewish Historical Society of Greater New Haven Archives.

PAGE 21 Postcard courtesy of Joe Taylor. Text sources: http://www. newenglandhistoricalsociety. com/s-z-poli-italian-immigrant-horrified-yankees/; http://connecticuthistory.org/sylvester-poli-negotiating-cultural-politics-in-an-age-of-immigration/; http://www.comune.coreglia.lu.it/ wp-content/uploads/2016/04/Il_Giornale_di_Coreglia_Marzo_2016.pdf; http://www.filmsite. org/1927-filmhistory.html; *New Haven Register*, December 22, 1954.

PAGE 22 Photo of theater courtesy of New Haven Museum. Photo of S.Z. Poli courtesy of Colin Caplan from his book *Legendary Locals of New Haven*. Text sources: http://www. newenglandhistoricalsociety.com/s-z-poli-italian-immigrant-horrified-yankees/; http:// connecticuthistory.org/sylvester-poli-negotiating-cultural-politics-in-an-age-of-immigration/; http:// www.comune.coreglia.lu.it/wp-content/uploads/2016/04/Il_Giornale_di_Coreglia_Marzo_2016. pdf; http://www.filmsite.org/1927-filmhistory.html; *New Haven Register*, December 22, 1954.

PAGE 23 Map credit: "The City of New Haven, Conn. 1879," created and published by O. H. Bailey and J.C. Hazen, Boston, c. 1879; Photo courtesy of *Centenary Souvenir Program, St. John's Roman Catholic Church 1834-1934*. Text: CT Irish American Historical Society Archives source, *History of the Diocese of Hartford* by Rev. James H. O'Donnell, 1900.

PAGE 24 Photo courtesy of New Haven Museum. Text source: CT Irish American Historical Society.

PAGE 25 Photos courtesy of New Haven Museum and CT Irish American Historical Society Archives, gift of Rita Hughes. Text source: CT Irish American Historical Society.

PAGE 26 Photo source: *B'nai Jacob One Hundred Years*, Jewish Historical Society Archives. Text sources: Margo Taylor, Chair Dixwell Church History Committee, and Jewish Historical Society of Greater New Haven Archives.

PAGE 27 Photo courtesy of Knights of Columbus. Text sources: Knights of Columbus and CT Irish American Historical Society.

PAGE 28 Photos courtesy of Jewish Historical Society of Greater New Haven Archives and New Haven Museum. Text source: Jewish Historical Society of Greater New Haven Archives.

PAGE 29 Photo courtesy of Joe Taylor. Text source: Elizabeth Brown, *New Haven: A Guide to Architecture and Urban Design*.

PAGE 30 Goode photos and text: Archives of the CT Irish American Historical Society, gift of Patricia Sanders Behan. DeDominicis text and photo courtesy of DeDominicis Family, John Migliaro and http://interactives-origin.wtnh.com/photomojo/gallery/19301/346942/ web-extra-uncle-aldo-dedominicis-photos/celebrating-a-unique-man/.

PAGE 31 Photo and text courtesy of Jewish Historical Society of Greater New Haven Archives.

PAGE 32, 33 Photo and text: *St. Michael's Ukrainian Catholic Church of New Haven 75th Jubilee Book*, 1984.

PAGE 36 Photo courtesy of New Haven Museum. Text source: Aaron Goode.

PAGE 37 Photo courtesy of New Haven Museum. *Souvenir Program from Grand Opening of the New Haven Arena* courtesy of Joe Taylor. Text source: Jewish Historical Society of Greater New Haven Archives.

PAGE 38 Photo and text courtesy of Jewish Historical Society of Greater New Haven Archives.

PAGE 39 Postcard courtesy of Joe Taylor. Text source: Jewish Historical Society of Greater New Haven Archives.

PAGE 40 Photos courtesy of the CT Irish American Historical Society Archives and *The Day* (New London, CT), June 7, 2015 (AP Photo). Text source: CT Irish American Historical Society.

PAGE 41 Photo courtesy of Aaron Goode. Text source: Jewish Historical Society of Greater New Haven Archives.

PAGE 42 Photo courtesy of Aaron Goode. Text source: Jewish Historical Society of Greater New Haven Archives.

PAGE 43 Photos courtesy of Knights of Columbus and CT Irish American Historical Society Archives, *History of the Knights of Columbus* by William O'Neill. Text source: *History of the Diocese of Hartford* by Rev. James H. O'Donnell, 1900, CT Irish American Historical Society Archives.

PAGE 44 Photos and text courtesy of Aaron Goode and Jewish Historical Society of Greater New Haven Archives.

JUN - 2017

Made in the USA
San Bernardino, CA
31 May 2017